Fear of the Unknown
Learning to laugh at the beauty of pain

Sidney Rigden

Copyright © 2024 Sidney Rigden

All rights reserved. No part of this book may be reproduced or transmitted in any form or by any means, electronic or mechanical, including photocopying, recording or by any information storage and retrieval system without permission in writing from the publisher.

Warrior Garden Literature, The—WI Rapids, WI
ISBN: 979-8-218-54322-8
Library of Congress Control Number: 2024923143
Fear of the Unknown: Learning to laugh at the beauty of pain
Author: Sidney Rigden
Digital distribution | 2024
Paperback | 2024

Published in the United States by New Book Authors Publishing

Thank Yous

First, I want to thank my children for making me want to be a better person, actually today, the 21st of May 2024, 6 years ago is when we had our gender reveal for our baby boy, Colton James, An American Hero. You, Colton, are the reason I knew I needed to try, for you. You are the sunlight in my universe, I am writing this in part to you son, so hopefully you will understand a little bit better than I did with your grandfather.

My sour patch, my ride or die, my daddy's girl, Rylee Rose. Rylee, you are hilarious, beautiful, strong, determined. You have the beauty and laughter of your mother and the strength and knowledge of your father. You have the support of all those that come before you and you will do amazing things for this world.

As I write this I am in the process of a separation from my wife, Cynthia, (this will help explain the true beauty of pain, as the book explains) one of the most beautiful women I have ever known or seen. You have provided life. I am sorry for who I was and what we were, but our kids will be great. I thank you for being a universe and creating our two babies, for that I have a love for you that will never leave. I will always help you with these crazy babies and I will always protect you to the best of my abilities.

I want to thank my brother, Shayne for coming into this world when I was nine years old and saving my life. Even though we live a different path, we still are best friends and you can always make me laugh. Thank you, we are so proud of you.

To my cousin Marty, you played the role of older brother, we fought, I blamed something on you, ran and you got in trouble. You took me under your wing, so many times. We deployed. We are not as close as we used to be, but now closer than ever. Thank you for always knowing when you need to be there for me.

Thank you, Kimberly and Jess, for being my "big sisters," even when you were being witches.

To my other aunts and uncles, near or far, you have played a role in raising me as a child or as a man. I love you.

To my Uncle Marty, you were the epitome of what a man was to me. You worked hard, provided, gave yourself to those around you, but stayed content most of the time, simply being happy in your surroundings.

Mom, thanks for loving books and giving birth to me, and raising a strong child. Dad, thank you for giving me your knowledge.

My three grandparents that are no longer here anymore, but here more than ever helping me write this book through life lessons.

Thank you to Eric, Eric and Derrick. Thank you to the Ann's. Brian. Thank you, Alex and Chris, Dyl Dyl. Thank you to my veteran brothers, you know who you are (remember I am here for you). To Dustin and Jess and all of their babies. Thank you to those that have left and caused me pain. HK Nick.

To all of my doctors, therapists and professional influences in my life that gave me tools for my toolbox whether you knew it or not, because I was listening, I was learning, I was making myself understand. I knew when to accept or when to make change, even when those choices included medications and lifestyle changes. I could see what you were doing right for me and I could see when you were just following a script, with all of the knowledge of your past, I gained some of this information from you, for the good or the bad, but all the better for me.

Last but not least, Gramma, you are the best person on Earth and I don't think you know that enough, you are the family rock, you taught me to be strong and level. Besides your faith I don't know how you do it. You only see the best in people, even when the demons/bad energy whatever you want to call it has them in their worst spot. I cannot simply say thank you, none of your family can. But thank you Gramma, we love you so much. Thank you for being our lighthouse.

Introduction

My entire life I have always wondered. I wondered what the stars were made of. I wondered which religion was the *true* religion, or the closest version of the truth. I even wondered why music had the ability to make certain people feel the way that they do and why music has the power to bring us together. I feel as though I looked at the sky and questioned the entire universe and all that it has to offer. I did not realize that coincidences in my life would continue to show me that there is always a new subject to learn, a new perspective, or point of view to explore in my life or another's.

From across the United States all the way to the Middle East, I learned many different perspectives about life. Yet, I did not fully understand the wisdom and messages I was given at the time.

I went to Sunday school with my grandmother. Sometimes it felt, I went to church for her, more than I did for myself. I don't recall learning a specific message, but I'm sure I had fun in the classroom with the other kids. In high school I went to youth group with my girlfriend because her uncle was the pastor. I really liked him and some of the other adults, they really could show me a different message I never found in church. Still they never answered my deepest questions with anything more than a "because," and I knew they could also not understand my question to the full extent because I had trouble translating my imagination into words sometimes. I stayed around a bit because I just liked the people around me but there was no spiritual comfort or feeling there.

All through life I have chased the symbols of the world beyond our own. Since the beginning I have had a love for movies that my father has given to me. One of the first people I remember because of him is Bruce Lee. I loved the power of a man that Bruce Lee presented to me in that time. I loved him as a person, but I did not understand him as a person, and I understood his movies as just that, entertainment.

While chasing the idea of what is or what is not life, I began to question the meaning of the Yin and the Yang. Trying to understand the philosophies of those across the world that I had some strange attraction or calling to. Something that gave me more in common with someone I normally would not, next door or across the world. I wanted to hear their perspective and in hearing it, I wanted to make sure I could translate that to myself as an understanding, leading me to a new perspective.

Through this symbol, the Yin and the Yang, I learned to realize it as just that, a symbol, it means nothing to my actual, everyday life, or does it? Through that symbol I found Bruce Lee in my life once again. This time as a philosopher. As I continue to understand the man he was, as I continue learning to become the better version of myself. I see the coincidences in life that are not coincidences. They are the life we are meant to find, even when it causes hardships for others, even when with pure heart we do not mean it to.

As I begin to see my life, in the way I believe Bruce Lee viewed his life, family and job. I believe Bruce

Lee also had this feeling I had and that is why he became as popular as he wanted. I think Bruce Lee realized the truth that very few do, I think he realized, and felt the path I was on, as he was also on one, and that he hit a certain point. Some call this Heaven, Nirvana, Enlightenment, Awakening or experiencing The Tao. But a Tao that can be explained is not the Tao. We are all saying the same word but only a few actually understand the feeling he was trying to explain to you. He comes from more of a basis of Taoism and Buddhism, because where he is from. Just as it is simpler to explain this feeling of my own with a general basis of Christian understanding, due to where I was born and raised. The feeling we are attempting to get across translates the same despite the words used.

A feeling, that I will do my absolute best to prove to you is possible, if you listen. I do not mean a feeling that any one thing can truly bring you or show you. You may have an idea, but it is nothing that proclaims worship. I found the feeling of what the world would typically describe as the word god, when I worked harder on my life than I ever have. When I started forcing myself to fix my own life. When I took responsibility for my actions. When I started seeing the good in myself. When I started accepting others and myself for what we are. When I started seeing the good in others by understanding their perspectives. When I began having more good days than bad. When I had nothing drawing to my soul in a good or bad light. Nothing emotionally draining or exciting. Nothing physically challenging.

I found God, in myself. The feeling is real. The symbol behind it means nothing. The person that may be behind it wanted you to know that the power is in you, not somewhere else. When you look into yourself, no matter how hard you, too will become closer to your true meaning. This takes time. This takes work. This takes effort. This takes pain. But, the moment of realization, is worth all the pain of the past. I can only try to prove to you that I found that feeling and you can as well. This is not a "self-help" book, but I truly hope it helps. This is a philosophical guide to finding yourself again. I am just a regular man who worked really hard to get a family back, to be the change he was supposed to be for them. Only to realize, they were already gone. Through this duality of life, I will help explain to you that the standard idea of god is not real, but that feeling is. If you pay attention, listen, ask questions and be open with yourself as well as with others. You will find that spark as well. Do not worry about who Bruce Lee is to me, he is only a symbol, however maybe understanding someone you do not know may open your mind on your journey. Be water, my friend.

As you read this, I simply ask that you read this with no bias to any thoughts of the life you have already created. Clear your mind from outside influence and imagine this is the first piece of information you have ever read. Read this with the curiosity of a philosopher but the imagination of a child. Like you are in a random desert and come across an ancient civilization and found this book laying alone in nothing else but stone ruins. Do not read this in a rush. Slow down, you have nowhere to be but here. People will find more importance in different areas. Read into everything, think about everything that you may see a similarity to, and why you have that similarity attached to this statement. Does it bring you sadness or happiness?

Why does it bring you the feelings it brings you, is it from a memory? Take your time, relive this moment, understand why it meant what it did to you, what could have gone better or worse, how could you have changed it? Could you have changed it? Would you have changed it. Read this from your own perspective, after that from the perspective of someone close to you or maybe someone you do not understand at all. Understand it, translate your own meaning to everything in here. Once you do this, do it again for those that came before you, then again for those that come after you.

I ask you to understand the words on the pages from your perspective to get a better understanding of your own self and consequently a better understanding of others. I would like you to question yourself in why that is a question to you. The deeper we think to the root of a question, the more we will find. We may even find the answer in the deepest, darkest areas of our lives. Often times people find change in the exact opposite areas in life of who they assumed they were supposed to be. Lost in a place they were supposed to be for others, not who they were supposed to be for themselves. Through understanding ourselves, it gives us additional tools to be able to understand others in the life we live.

My name is Sidney Rigden, at this point in my life I feel as if I have lived 1000 lives. I can understand the things taught to me through all of my life on a different level that I did not think was possible. Things I did not remember or I found insignificant. In my first adult life I was trained to take a life. In my second adult life I was trained to save a life. In my new life, I will continue to help others, and I will do it in a new light. Grateful of the opportunity to help those around me.

In what I feel is the strongest version of each of these, I have lost and I have won. I have lost and I have found. I have loved and I have hated. I have sat in a pew and I have sat in the woods. I have worked with doctors, healers and those between them. I have walked in the dark alone and I have found those few in my life that truly are here from a place of genuine love for me when I could not see it before. I've sat and wondered what my parents did right or wrong, what their parents did right or wrong and all of those before.

I have had the worst thoughts imaginable, however, the ones I cannot imagine, I cannot live without.

I am writing this to you in the hopes of adding to your tool box of life. If just one small thing in this book creates any meaning in your life and helps make a positive change for you or others, then I have already succeeded and I thank you for allowing me to help. With that said, do not chase symbols, ideas, or structures built around something you do not understand. Create your own symbols in life, then use it to succeed and tell others what it meant to you and exactly why. Chances are that small symbol already means nothing to them, but hopefully it does, or sparks their brain into understanding another point of view.

I am writing this because there is so much knowledge in this world that so many do not know is available. Some simply do not wish to understand and for their own lack of understanding find a blame or fear in another person's way of life. Take this book and understand the learning provided from it came from hundreds of generations of wisdom. From people that genuinely were interested in asking "why?" From people that were not afraid to be different and question what is seen as normal by the masses. Those with good intuition, knowledge and a strong analytical sense. The more perspectives you can understand in your life and the life of the others, the more you will begin to understand others around the world.

Although many great men and women have written on similar things that I will cover, it is my hope that this book has a different audience, those that feel broken. The ones that feel like they cannot go on but know they need to, even though they think do not have a reason. If all of the hours and lifetimes of pain going into this book help, it is worth it. If it helps more than one, in the smallest way, then some would call that magick. The last thing I hope this book accomplishes is that it brings people to the other strong thinkers, translators for the world before myself, the greats like Marcus Aurelius, Dr. Seuss, Allen Watts, Manly P. Hall, Mike Ness, Anthony Bourdain, HP Blavatsky, Sebastian Junger, Carl Jung, Lao Tsu, Bruce Lee and so many more that have brought generations of pain and knowledge to the world and myself. I would love to imagine that this book was found through them, even though I would never put myself into a category anywhere close to any of them in their fields.

Most humans from the beginning want the same thing, happiness. We all experience pain, some more than others. However, so many people do not chase true love through happiness because of the universes that were built around them. The structured programming society brings. Not everyone is ready for college, not everyone wants to go to college, not everyone wants to be a parent, some people unfortunately cannot. We are told to chase everything but our own dreams. Just like as a child when we may have the privilege to chase our dream, maybe sometimes we lose the love there but we are so scared to bring it up because I have already invested so much time, or my parents invested too much or my coach or instructor. We are fitting into what is considered normal in someone else's life and not fitting our own, so much so that we become lost in the cosmos, the stars, in our own head. We seem to be living in a constant loop with no real change.

Being lost here can lead to a majority of mental health disorders including anxiety and depression. As well as having a terrible diet, excessive alcohol intake or anger issues. If we stop using our entire brain, if we do not exercise our body the way it is meant to be, and if we do not eat the way we should power our mind, body and soul, we will not feel happy or content in some form. In each of these ways of life, there must be a balance to provide our true happiness.

Being lost in this place, this most useless place, without noticing it will continue to wind up your soul or mind, worsening your anger and anxiety, or possibly making you cry for no reason. Inside you are lost and do not understand how or why. You are confused in the loop of life you are in. Where can you slowly begin to make changes?

In this book, if I can give you the smallest glimmer of "how or why" then I know you will succeed on your journey. Maybe your journey just began, maybe you feel it is coming to an end or somewhere in between. Wherever you are on your journey, you are here now, thank you for being with me. If you fully understand this book, maybe you know the feelings I have felt. Maybe I do not have the words you understand to translate that feeling in this book for you. Either way, I wish you nothing but happiness in your life and I am honored, no, I am grateful to have you here in this moment, with me.

Now please listen to the words I place on these pages, please understand and feel my intention behind every word I type, make your own interpretation. Use your brain, train your brain, expand your brain. Sometimes the journey gets very hard, sometimes it will get harder again without you knowing it, however, soon you will be able to create your future instead of trying to predict it, by being present in your own life. But I truly hope this finds you when it is supposed to, to give you the comfort you may need or to confirm a coincidence. I am only writing this because I care about you, I want you to have a better life. I want you to feel love in everything you cherish. Because love is happiness. Hear me when I tell you this, do not overthink it, I care about you, in the most ancestral basic human way, I care.

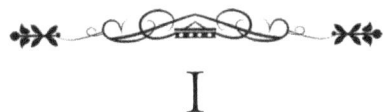

I

What I have come to learn is that everyone wants to be heard, but no one wants to talk, in fear of being wrong or by not being someone else's version of normal. But, how can we come together as humans if at the same time, nobody wants to listen to each other either?

We are different, we are supposed to be different. Every single child that is born, will be like nobody else. So how can we properly raise a child, we cannot, because as a parent, we are the first version of ourselves, just as our children are the first versions of their selves, there is no book, there is only righteousness. Creating the best version of yourself, leads to the best versions of those that come after us. Righteousness is an idea that you would see across multiple areas, as being a good person.

What is a good person? What defines good and bad? To understand the good and the bad we must break down the deepest roots of our self to figure out what one we are. We all have good in us, just as we can all have bad in multiple forms. The things we may lie about because it brings us feelings of shame. Shame that we do not understand the origin of. Have we thought about why this one thing causes me any sort of shame. Maybe the things in your life that you take the most shame in, are where your answers are. It takes a lot of time and effort to figure yourself out, but in this process, you begin to understand the way another may view you. Answering who was right or wrong, what was good or bad. Or, understanding it was not your fault and it was not their fault. Agreeing to compromise along the way. Acceptance.

Accept yourself as you see you. Accept yourself as others see you. Accept others the way you see them. Accept others the way they see you. Even the bad.

When I say the best version of yourself, I am not asking how much money you make or the things you own, I want to ask you, "Are you happy?" Happiness comes in a variety of forms as long as we allow it. Happiness is good grades in college because you want to be a doctor so you can make a positive difference in the world. Happiness can be getting the perfect picture you have been working so hard for. Happiness is teaching your child how a weapon works. Happiness is creating music for others. Happiness is go-karts. Happiness can be anything, what things make you honestly happy?

This is where it gets hard. We know where our happiness lays, we just need to ask. The person with this answer is often found to be our inner child, so how do we ask them? Thinking. Thinking to yourself, in the quiet, in the woods, near a river, on your favorite trail, or on a mountain. If you do not have a form of Earth that pulls at your soul, search for one. Find a way to meditate. Meditation does not have to be sitting in front of a tree, legs crossed eyes closed. Meditation can start at any place you can actually calm your mind, maybe it allows you to think about issues at hand or maybe it brings complete silence to your mind. The world around us is usually so busy and loud that if we allow it to, we will not find peace and quiet for ourselves.

Finding that meditative state may be a bit more challenging to some, but it comes from some form of passion, so if you just might happen to notice a surrounding that does this to your mind, notice it, understand it, why here, why now. Some people can completely quiet their mind, while they are hearing and feeling the thunder of race cars in front of them, to some it's on the top of a high dive board. If you are not sure where yours is, enter nature by yourself and no distractions. The trees, the water, the wind, may just give you the next clue in your life. Do not attempt to explore, or figure out the nature, just be there, be part of it, have a rest and listen. Simply enjoy the moment.

Sports, music and other entertainment are ok to find a priority in as long as we understand what they do for us. That will show you where that priority should lay. If we are happy at home are we happy at work. Does entertainment affect a friendship. Through our priorities, we create a balancing act in all things that are part of us.

When we maintain a perfect balance in our life, we can reach a point that we will always chase, while showing people who we actually are. You and others will watch your success by your actions.

When I use the word righteousness, I speak only to the understanding of the world before me that covers most of the global religions or philosophies. Areas I may have a wealth of knowledge or others I may have less knowledge in. I speak of righteousness in a way that is to make you understand that murder is the ultimate sin in a spiritual sense. What if yourself or someone around you was about to be put in a situation that may cause their life at the hand of another and you defend yourself, is this still a sin? Explain why, if you do not understand that other person and their actions. Using words such as "crazy" or "lost" are not a true reason someone is who they become, as the issue is often much deeper than you understand or are willing to understand. Labeling someone else without understanding and actually knowing them is weak and lazy, this shows only your own downfalls. From countries, to religion, to politics, to your neighbor. Do not throw rocks.

I mean being someone that helps someone in need. This does not mean helping everyone that asks. This is where you begin to see your boundaries, or priorities. You give to someone the exact same amount that they give you. Sometimes for those we love we know we have to give more to them at times. Sometimes they can give more of themselves for us. This means helping someone that you love with every tool you have available at the time.

I mean living your life in a way that gives back to those around you. Those that have always been there for you. In your social life, in your career, in your schooling and in your personal life. The people that really mean something to you even if you are not close. Wherever these important people come from, remember them along the way. As your journeys begin to connect, for any reason, you will begin to notice the importance of that person, whether they stay in your life or not. This is why we do not judge others.

As you begin living your life in a way that you believe is good to you and those around you. You begin to find the things in your life important to you. The meaning behind them and what they mean to you. We begin to see the world in a different way that could bring a positive change to this world. We see this through art in the broadest sense and through forms of science. We see this through literature (so please listen). We can see this in any way our heart chooses to take us. It takes us that way for good and to do good, promising a successful path along the way as long as you make the effort with no excuses. If you see the big picture of your dreams, you need to use your skills to start putting the puzzle pieces together and then figuring out what you will do after it is complete. and then figuring out what you will do after it is complete. and then figuring out what you will do after it is complete.

Success chased in the form of gold is where the dragon is found. As we search for our way in life, we need to practice making a conscious effort to make sure the thing that can bring us to a higher place in life, will only do so through the help of others and staying true to yourself. Understanding and thanking those along the way, while you continue to help pull them through as well, in any way you can. The more similar another person's priorities are to your own, the easier it is to establish a foundation of trust with that person.

If this person wrongs you in the end, why did you allow that to happen? What were you blinded by that removed your mind from what it should be feeling? What were you allowing that created different forms of unhappiness in you? Do not invest into others what you cannot afford.

Obviously, we feel that we can find this in another person, the butterflies are our heart, but is it our heart speaking through our nervous system? What is drawing me to this person. Why do I feel such when I am with them. What about them is different. Do they still have similar morals and priorities to you? Are you able to have all forms of communication with that person and not feel like less of a person yourself, or making the other person feel that way? If you feel a disconnect on either side, where is this coming from? Is this happening from a lack of communication because the words are not known for the feelings. Are you able to speak with meaning and compassion to each other? Can you learn to. You must speak what you feel to those you love, or they may assume you do not feel that way. For good or bad.

Change is simple, not easy. The idea of actually following your heart is so foreign in these times. That is why it is not easy, it is a very painful process if you are becoming your true self. You lose friends, jobs, sometimes family in the journey. In the end you need to become yourself again to maintain a truly happy life.

There are times when you must deal with the pain, there are times you need to sit in the pain, we need to teach our body that there is nothing to be afraid of. This pain can be large pain or small pain. Pain is pain. In this moment, what are my basic needs and are they being met? This allows you to give yourself time to process the issue. This allows you time now to think about this issue. Find out why it is an issue and create a list of possible solutions available to you in the moment.

You need to have your mind open, no distractions. If there are distractions you may not be thinking clearly. You need to think about the problem by yourself with no outside influence. Let your mind talk, just like you want to. Slow down, understand, do not assume or jump to conclusions. This is the most basic form of miscommunication that can easily grow to a much larger problem. What is the situation worth to you? When you calm your mind, you can now focus on the issue at hand. You can do this for past issues, you can do this for things you may want to see happen in the future. You can learn to do this, in the moment. This is how you learn, the more you practice the more you understand.

You must understand the feelings that come along with being an animal. Your brain, heart and gut will send signals to each other and to the rest of your body. In times of stress we must realize this, that our body is just doing what it was created to do. To react to people, places and things in different ways. When we allow certain things to control enough of us mentally, we become its slave. You can see people addicted to many things, including their friends, family, sports, food, technology, and the list goes on. Just because it is a person, not a drug, does not mean it is not an addiction in the basic sense to your animal brain.

If you are in a situation that seems chaotic and cannot manage the fear of pain in that moment, why did you put yourself in that situation? Is this the fear of a new job or relationship? Maybe the fear of losing a job or somebody. What effort are you putting in to understand that fear behind your feelings. This fear may give you the reason to leave, perhaps the reason to stay. This also applies to other places in life. If you do not feel comfortable somewhere, do not go there unless you are prepared. If you are not prepared, explain to yourself why. Can you become better prepared for this situation? Can this situation wait until you are better prepared. If there is a reason to go there, is it worth it. If you are prepared, take your step, you have already done the hard work, do not let the fear question your experience.

There is always a solution to your problem, an answer to your question, it is up to you to acknowledge it without judgement. Just because it was not your first option, does not mean you should waste energy being upset. Why are you angry at the answer you are given, are you afraid? Afraid of what? Should you be mad at the road when it slows your travels, maybe for a moment, but after that being honest with yourself, you realize you did not leave with enough time, you did not think of traffic, or you forgot you needed to add a spare tire. Maybe you did, but there was an accident or something broke. What can you do in this moment, realizing your basic needs are met, to think of a solution to this problem. We must not view the world we live in as a place that will always cater to us, to keep us safe. But we must do our best to cater for it and to keep others safe.

II

My father was not a righteous human, my whole life and passed his death I did not think much of him as a father. Now I understand, he was incredibly smart, he just did not know how to translate his feelings to others. He was misunderstood. He chased the feelings he couldn't explain with drugs until they killed him. If it wasn't for my father always asking me the really big "why" questions, I wouldn't have always loved a bonfire under the stars as a child. Meaning I never would have written this book. I would not have the brain power to translate the thoughts of generations into this compressed version of many thoughts and ideas into who and what we are as human souls. Something small, that I never noticed the significance of in my life, was enjoying a simple fire under the sky, and saying, "What if?"

What if we follow what we love? Things will come naturally, because it will lead you to your tribe. We are a tribal animal in a human race. Your passion for the things you do, will bring you to others with the same passion. I say passion, as a different word for love. I want you to understand the difference between a hobby and a passion. We all chase hobbies, we spend our hard earned energy to work to pay for a new hobby only to find out we didn't really care for it. Passions are different, passions are what we chase that makes our soul truly happy. Something that you teach yourself every aspect of because you simply love learning, growing, seeing, and experiencing whatever that thing is. It is not a chore, it is not a job, it is a passion.

This is also why some things we look at doing, we find joy in, but want to keep the joy at home, we do not wish this to be our job, it is where we can think. If one finds gardening therapeutic, find out why they feel that way about it. In the end there is a return to you in the form of food. Maybe while making your own food, you have time to relax. Maybe for you that is making a chair to sit. Making art for friends. This is the difference between a passion and a hobby. Some hobbies and passions could become successful if you would like that. You know what you could do to make it work, it may be hard, but can you do it?

If you chase your passion, and truly chase it with no excuses of what you can and cannot do, you will succeed, when you succeed, you will live a happy, content, comfortable life. Once you start chasing gold, you will take yourself off track, further from happiness. The reason you find these passions are from those before you that had a real passion for it that they wished to teach you, maybe not, maybe you simply were curious and found your own thing, the thing that got your mind working in the beginning. Perchance you are still searching for that thing. Follow your heart not your mind, be responsible where you need to be and most importantly, be safe.

I understand that money simply can buy happiness, sometimes it can, when we are down and want to see a show or we are behind financially, but money will always come and go, stop chasing materials and chase passions, because then, as long as you refuse to make an excuse, you will succeed. Chances are that others are also interested in our passion, just maybe not to the point we are. That is ok, if they simply enjoy it for what it is, then you have done it. Do not tell them all of the effort that went into it, unless they are genuinely curious.

We make money an issue for ourselves through the choices we make in our lives. Money is a material possession. I have worked overtime most of my life, I understand this struggle. I also understand the position I place myself in, when overbuying such as eating out, going to events that require money when a free park may be good enough or simply buying too much house. Again, life is perspectives, stop chasing what others have and what you think they have. What do you need now. Everyone struggles on and off. The house you do not want, will not always be your house. Give it time and effort, but thank the home for the time it sheltered you. Hard times build strong people, you did it, stay humble.

Maybe you have had a passion for most of your life and you are still actively in that passion, but you don't love it as much as you used to. Do you still love it enough to keep doing it because it provides for you? Can you continue to do this while you train for the next passion? We can chase many dreams. Some dreams may come true, some dreams we achieve give us just enough to go on in the real world, so we can chase a different passion in life. Unfortunately, some dreams just do not come true. Was it a realistic dream? Can you honestly tell yourself you did everything in your will to make it happen? You know the answer to that, not me, be true to yourself. Sometimes dreams we are living, end. Sometimes it hurts, really bad. Really, really bad. Let it hurt, but observe yourself on the inside and observe the world around you, what is next? Find the other dream or passion. Move on to the next mission. Live all of your lives until you find peace, a place where you can be safe and happy.

When you start living your passion, you begin to realize that anything can be a metaphor for life. In racing, where is the balance between stop and go. In photography you need to give up light for speed or speed for light. You start to see the beauty in the thing you are doing and understanding why it makes you happy. It is that simple, let it make you happy in that moment.

Sometimes we are unsure where our hidden passions lay, so we must look back throughout our lives. Sometimes it's very hard to understand our inner self, maybe even our inner child or teenager, what did we not get to do that we always felt we wanted or needed to do? Still, as adults we talk down to our inner child when we say we cannot do something we may enjoy, because of the time of day, the finances, or simply because of our own mood. You shut yourself down, you shut the child inside of you down. That never felt good as a kid, why do it to yourself now? When you are telling yourself no, is it worth the sacrifice? Sometimes you need to treat yourself, but not enough that it is no longer a treat. If we have proper balance in our lives, we become a better friend, a better worker, a better person, a better parent.

In the things you do and love, become your biggest fan, coach yourself through the corners in only a way you can. Only you can actually feel the experience that is happening. Be excited for the incredible picture of the stars you captured. Do a victory dance for solving an equation. By forcing yourself to be happy in what you are doing, even if you do not mean it in the moment, your brain will change. When your brain begins to change, your life will begin to change.

Life can get very dark at times. But understand the duality of life, with bad will come good. The more energy you put in to one item, the more energy can be taken from you by that item, or given to you. This is why we stay grateful and appreciate that person or item in life and what it does for us. As long as that mindset is always there, chances are, it will stay.

We all speak about it, but less of us chase it because we think we already know what it is. Happiness is the best feeling in the world, happiness is love. Some of us do know what happiness is, because of the generations before us allowed for us a simple life, a happy life with almost perfect balance, but if that is you, most likely you would not be reading this, either way. Thank you.

III

As you slowly begin to change, if you have not already, you will begin to set up boundaries. Some people have none, some people have too many. If you are someone that has a hard time with this, it's understandable. Most of us want to make other people feel comfortable, it's hard to say no. Soon this will become much easier for you.

This may be a very foreign place to you, but do not be afraid, this is healing. This is bringing you back to your true self. Yes, sometimes we must actually do things that we do not want to, but we do it because we happily will give our energy to that person to make them happy. We do not need to give our energy to people or things that do not restore it. When we do the things we do not want to do, for those we care about and they care about us as well, they will give back to you in some way to bring you happiness. Otherwise there is no balance and without balance that friendship, relationship or group may just eventually end to you. It can end in pain or it can fade away. If our boundaries are too strong, others may view us in a darker light as something they do not understand even when you want to help. If our boundaries are very weak, we often have trouble getting ourselves or others out of a tough spot. Find your tribe and learn to talk to others, learn to open up and talk. Save yourself.

You should not feel bad about establishing boundaries. You owe it to yourself to do things that bring you happiness. If other people do not like this, you need to be happy going with yourself, perhaps meeting others with the shared interest along the way. Do not let others take away from your excitement for something. Go by yourself and if they are mad, then that is their own fault. Why should they be angry at you for doing something you enjoy and does not hurt them? Perhaps the answer to that is in them. And yes, sometimes some things are simply not possible in that moment, but how can you change that for the future version of you?

Most people refuse to understand that there are multiple solutions to all problems, some are simple, while some are not. However, having a backup plan is always a simple action you can make to alleviate the possible anxiety of what may come up on your trip.

When someone offers you a solution, do not be prideful and deny their help. Why would you not want someone to help you? If someone willingly wants to help you, that means in some way they care, it does not matter to what extent. Let people care. If you call for help, do not refuse it. Do not refuse to be wrong. Be coachable. Always be humble.

If you can figure out something faster than me, please do so, I may be able to learn from this experience and see how I can do it different next time. If I can do it faster or easier, please allow me, I mean no disrespect, it's simply something I know and understand, let me show you.

When someone is speaking, please listen to their words, feel their intentions, and simply let them finish. Do not speak over them or shut them down. Someone is attempting to create words, their brain is processing what they are trying to say. Sometimes they may ask for help, maybe asking "what's their name" or "what's this called." Otherwise let them finish, by stepping over them, even when they may be talking too slow for you,

you are undermining them, even if you do not mean to be. They know what they are trying to say, let the brain exercise a little bit and listen, you are not in a rush.

This same applies for children, they are still learning vocabulary. If your child is a toddler, a teenage or an adult, let them speak. They do not know all the ways of words the way you understand them. Let them search, watch them think about it, get excited that their brain is working and they are thinking. Obviously, sometimes with this, you may offer them a simpler word or explanation that they do not understand. Take it slow, teach them or learn with them.

When someone is constantly spoken over or shut down, they may take this in a way that makes them feel like they are less of a person. If they know they are intelligent and are not allowed to speak, they may shut down, they may become angry, they may become sad. These actions are the reactions to our past. If someone is constantly being spoken over by a single person, they will believe that they are not as smart as that person, or simply grow to hate that person if they do not understand each other, possibly a subconscious hate that they are not aware of. Sometimes we know that you mean no harm by it and were simply trying to help, but once that has happened and the conversation has moved on, I no longer have the chance to tell you that I knew the answer, I was just trying to articulate the way my thoughts became words so you would understand. Sometimes I do not know, and that is when I would like your help. I truly appreciate the knowledge you may be able to give me in this moment. Sometimes the slowest ones to respond can give you the best answer.

Understanding boundaries before going into a relationship can save you a large amount of pain. Because when you meet this person, they get the real version of you. They do not get the old version of you. They do not get the new version of you. They simply get you. As long as they love you for who you are, you are already achieving success. This is why we must understand our boundaries. This builds a strong relationship. Priorities and boundaries in any relationship are the closest way to be true to yourself.

So, stop chasing relationships. Everyone wants someone. Let it happen. If you do not let it happen, it cannot. As you follow your dreams, the people who will love you, will be in the area already. People keep struggling to find love because they are doing it in the wrong places, physically or mentally. This does not mean you have to meet someone at a bar, church or grocery store. It means they will be in the psychology class you are really excited to take, in the kayaking group you decided to join or maybe they are in the pew behind you. In some way their priorities are aligned with yours. Figure out what else they like. Your opportunity will present itself, then, be yourself with them and see if their plans co-align with yours in a way that is comfortable to you both. This will help lead you to success in life and love.

If you are already in a relationship that you feel you want to be in with all of your being, then I say to you "congrats" I am extremely happy for you, consider yourself lucky, even if it took a lot to get there, do not take it for granted, be grateful every day. If you have kids, you still need your own time. Agree for a balance with your partner to make sure your passions can still be done, alone or shared. Happily, with no judgement on who is gone and who is with the children, because the children are the greatest gift we are given. That does not take away from the fact that we still need our own time, to do our version of clearing our mind.

Many parents find it difficult balancing how much they need to invest in their child. Some parents come from a different upbringing and they push their child to do their best, so much that the child eventually loses their passion because the parent overstepped. Now the child is looking for a different joy in life because you took theirs away.

Some parents do not support enough. Their priorities may not be aligned to their children's passions. They may care more about spending money on trivial items while telling their child learning to play the saxophone, piano or guitar is silly or a waste of time and money.

Some parents walk a very fine line. If my kid loves this, and wants to be the best, how do I make them become the best. Simple, let them. If you can afford to do so obviously, but if you truly cannot, your child will understand. Maybe they see the hard work they are putting into this, as they see all the hard work you are putting in to them.

If any of the words in this book make you feel anything positive, I hope this changes your views on children, the children who never had a chance to succeed because of the life that was created before them. Just because they may of came from money or poverty does not mean they were shown the right way to live life true to themselves. And, I hope this changes your view on yourself, relax, we are all trying to succeed at different rates. I feel these words may help you enough to ensure the proper care of those that come after you, while understanding those before you. That you begin to view life as memories, not trying to predict the future.

IV

Do not count on your media to explain to you who others are. You simply must find out for yourself. There is so much disconnect in the world we live in that creates nothing but confusion for us, confusion leads to fear, fear leads to anxiety.

The less that people talk to each other and understand one another, the world begins to slowly end over time. People in other cultures have things that they love, that is unique to their culture, and when somebody truly loves something, they want to share it with you and expect nothing in return other than to see their passion bring you happiness. Of course, we may still stick to our own tribe, but that doesn't mean we cannot be friends with the tribe over. Maybe my tribe is completely efficient and content in their lives. Your people may have a product that may help others. Others may have a product that may help you. If your values align with each other, you may be able to grow a larger community, together or apart.

That is not my tribe, no, but I got to sit with them, talk to them, explain something I love to them, we talked, we listened, we heard each other. In turn, we helped each other grow.

If we ignore and stay quiet, how can we answer our own questions? What is that tribe up to? Are they good or are they bad? Are they misunderstood? They also do not understand you. That doesn't mean running to the middle of the square and asking questions, it's about being curious, not afraid. If you see one of them on the trail and asking a question maybe you would like to know. Ask your questions from a place of genuine curiosity, not as a form of judgement. I am trying to understand you, because I want the world to understand everyone better.

We all come from a different area, just as we come from different parents. Just because your culture tells you what is right, does not mean that it is. Read for yourself, read their book, eat their food, sit at their table.

I will not be getting religious, but I will say people that understand what they see as the true meaning of faith, are generally good people, they live through books and stories filled with metaphors for living a good, proper, righteous life and they want that in others as well. There are those that do not understand the reason behind religion, the moral of the story, to love your neighbor, to not make judgements, to accept them as you accept yourself, if you have accepted yourself, most have not. Most refuse to try and place themselves in the life of another, because you simply can never be that person, but you can do your best to understand.

The child, loses his father to war. A war he knew nothing about, all he knew was this tribe killed his father, for what. Does this kid take revenge? If he does, does this make him a bad person? What if he chooses not to, is that the righteous way or is that a form of defeat? Life is all perspectives of those around you, and unless you ask, you will never come close to knowing the truth.

Yes, some people do not have good intentions. We do not associate with these people when we realize this, or do our best not to. Some people are simply selfish, they will find their way out of the tribe. Some people want the glory from the success of others. Know your audience and never trust someone as much as you trust yourself. You can trust, you should trust, but your heart knows their intentions to you, sometimes it doesn't work out. With loss comes gain, even when you do not see it.

Some people are misunderstood due to mental health or a social status. That is why we do not go certain places or eat at a certain place. Where did this danger begin though? Were they a happy child, did they have dreams, did they have a chance at success or not? Sometimes we do not know and we cannot find out, we simply accept some things as the way they are. But the more you talk to that person from the other tribe, the more you understand.

Our genes are strong, you cannot be mad at the soldier for going to war when he saw his heroes before him do the same. One that was raised to believe in their country, to believe in justice. To believe what they were raised to see as just. Just as you cannot blame the flower child who has disgust and hatred towards the soldier because they were raised around peace and love. Where is the balance here? If you are programmed for war as a child you have not been taught peace. If you were raised around peace and those before you did not train you properly, you are filled with fear by what is unknown or misunderstood, and that can create wars, even in your own head.

We refuse to understand each other, and that is our issue. The balance is finding your passions that lead you to a life where there can be no fear. You must become a warrior in the garden. You must know how to be a truly dangerous person, that is at peace with themselves. Without the peace comes anger and anger is fear. If we only see the world as a good place, refusing to believe there is bad around us, then we are not prepared to save ourselves. This leads to anxiety, anxiety is fear.

I am not contradicting myself saying that everyone wants to be good but some people do not have that intention. What I am saying is that some people you simply cannot save, it is not your job and some of those people are dangerous, emotionally or physically. We have so far to go in society and it starts with you. The more peace you can present to those around you, will lead to those asking you how you found it. This is what I hope I am doing for you through these words. The most powerful person in the world, has no fear because they have prepared their life, through good and bad. To be ready for anything they can control, and to simply understand most things they just have no control over. Pick and choose your battles with a total understanding of yourself and the other.

Is one wrong for explaining their bad day to the dying person? Pain is pain, of course people experience this on a spectrum, but that does not mean your pain is any worse than anyone else's. Can you still understand that persons pain through your own? Or is your pain more important? No, because pain hurts, we do not want to hurt. Maybe the dying man can offer incite as to why your pain, is not real pain to him, perhaps why he feels your pain is trivial. You do not feel it is trivial, take turns understanding why you both think that way. Allow yourself to alter your perspective, it may be for the better for both of you.

Sometimes pain comes in the form of death, but why? If this person I am losing means so much to me that is causes me pain? Why? Why does it cause me this pain, because this person gave me amazing memories, and for that I am not sad, I am thankful. This can lead to confusion, for moments that is ok. However, for that person that meant so much to you, you also meant that much to them. For that person you must continue. You go on to keep them alive, simply by living a happy, truthful life. Hell is here in the world we create, and it is up to us to not be there if we do not want to be. There is no one coming to save you but yourself, no matter how bad you want to believe someone else can take away your pain, they may only mask it. So, take a deep breath and think. Plan for the best, prepare for the worst. Live everyday creating the memories you want to remember. Make the memories of others good. They may not have very many.

Even when you are in a state of fear, let others help you if they have the ability. Maybe they have lived through this issue, or maybe they had to painfully watch another person with this issue, and through them, they have an answer for you.

This shows how connected we really are. This is more than spiritual, this is not a false persona of "one love." This is a truth you will see in your life if you allow it. Be wrong. Learn. Thank them for teaching you. When you say "I know" you are telling the person trying to help you that you are wasting their time.

V

Even the fun of events creates a divide if you let it and most do. Are you cheering for the person running their hardest, or just the person who is winning? Did the person running their hardest practice as much as the person winning, is the person winning just a genetic freak? Was the winner waking up before the sun for years prior to the other runner and has earned this run.

Let your entertainment be simply that, entertainment. Entertainment is not your life, it is the life of others. Others that you are giving your emotional energy to. That lost emotional energy in an already unbalanced life, can lead to an unstable spiral. If you have stability and can actually enjoy an event and not let it affect your life, then let it, there are many tribes in the forms of entertainment, but just listening to a song or watching a show will not heal you.

Finding your passions can help lead you to your tribes. If you go to a race car track you will find an entire group of people sharing the same passion. They will talk drivers with you, they will talk standings, they will embrace the power behind it and why it is so important to them. The same can be said for music festivals, sporting events, movie festivals and much more. Where do you want to learn? Where do you want to teach or guide?

During these events in your life for work, school or fun as you meet people along the way, certain people just stick out to us, this does not have to be romantic and does not necessarily mean good. Something about them you just like. Pretend we are all from the stars and we came to earth and everyone's soul landed in a different body around the world. These people are showing something to you, because somehow you know something about them, you can sense it. Maybe you have a similar story, maybe have a similar past or envision a similar future. Maybe that person is just the person that is always there for you. Are you always there for them?

Music is one of our oldest forms of communication. So, was older music actually better or worse? Did it just mean something different to that era of people then it does to those younger or older. What music did the important people in your life listen to. Have you tried listening to it? Were they trying to tell you something or were they trying to figure an issue out while they listened to their favorite music. Sometimes some music is just silly, not to say bad, but to say we do not care what went into it, for good or bad, this song makes me happy and I'm going to enjoy it.

We want our children, our friends, and our family to find their own music. A music we may have never known. Music that can translate a song into feelings for that person. Allowing them to communicate their feelings to us. We also want people to hear our music for this same reason. Why is this song important to me, why is it important to them? Some people in life will say they do not listen to music. Are they lost, or have they never been hurt?

Listen to different music, put yourself out there, do it by yourself if you need to. Use music to help get through tough spots and appreciate why it was written. Usually, the songs we go to when we are hurting, are written because someone else was hurting, that's some of the beauty of life. Their pain may of lead to their success, where they can help you deal with your pain.

One saying is to "make yourself comfortable being uncomfortable." Music is a very easy way for most to start this process. Try out the music you do not like, realize even though you may still not really like it, you understand it. This same thing applies to going for that hike, taking an art class, learning the proper use of a firearm, or trying that one awesome thing in life you want to try, but it is scary. Let it be scary, but do not let it scare you. Let the anxiety be the butterflies. Enjoy your jump.

Music can bring us together better than almost anything and that's why it is prevalent in all cultures and in all of them before us. This does not mean music has to be your life, let it be a part of your life. Let the song help heal you and appreciate it for what it did for you. Let the song make you dance. Some people want their music to make them feel happiness, some people want to feel the pain. Music drives your mood. Be thankful for that music. Listen to the music.

VI

Family is the most important thing in our life. If you feel you do not have a family, I do feel compassion for you. However, you most likely do have family, you are just not talking to them for whatever reason. If you can stop blaming that person, start understanding that person, you tell them sorry, mean it, say it with intention. If they refuse to see past this, there is nothing you can do. But at this point you understand them a little more, it does not hurt you as much, as now you simply would like to help them if you can.

If you have a strong family, you are blessed. Do not let outside relationships ruin this for you. As a child, make sure your family is priority, they want the best for you. You choose people that do not make you question your own family, someone that wants to see your family as much as their own. This creates a larger, healthier tribe. This raises stronger friendships in youth life, this raises stronger children, this creates happier parents.

Sometimes we feel like some friends are more family than actual family members. That is ok, it's great to have them people in your life. This is because nobody is the same person, but maybe their parents influenced them in just a way that your parents influenced your life, to make a perfect balance of friendship. Making you view that person as you would family. Make sure you keep that person, love their family and let them love yours. Maybe that person helps you create the family you have actually always wanted in your life.

One of the most painful things for a tribe can be losing a member, this affects the balance of the tribe. This may cause you to lose another family member. Leaving few if any. How do we stay together as a tribe when one member is lost. Why did we lose that member. Was there anything that we as a tribe could have done to keep that person here. Is there anything I could have done? If so, is this a change we are willing or able to make?

Having a strong tribe, leads to a strong lifestyle. Your tribe is there for you as you are there for them. The kids always have adults around, teaching them from their years of knowledge, keeping them safe, keeping them cared for. The older people have the younger ones to do the things they no longer can. And, they have you, to do all the things in between. The things the kids will soon be doing. This allows you more freedom to yourself. This allows you to love. This allows you enough freedom to continue to find yourself. This allows you to give back to those helping you. Allowing your continuous growth. For yourself and for the tribe.

VII

Who is right on the reason we are here? The secret is, that it does not matter. You can search for an answer with no solid evidence, but many strong ideas leading to it. How does one's theory of evolution then explain the bee or the common house cat? When we search for solutions that are meaningless to us, in our immediate life, we are creating problems. That is why we must focus on ourselves and those around us that we love.

This of course does not mean we cannot be curious. Of course we can, that is the meaning behind this book. Sometimes this is when we need to really understand the difference between a passion and a hobby. Am I pulling myself away from my actual priorities for this. What is making this a priority to me?

When you realize that you do not need your spirituality or religion to fully become the person you are meant to be, but realize the path they were trying to show you, it all makes perfect sense. This is where we become truly grateful. This is where we become truly powerful. Due to the work we have done ourselves, the work we have done for others, and the positive changes we can remember along the way.

Being religious does not make you a good person, it does not make you a bad person. Just as being a philosopher does not make you right or wrong. Same as a scientist. Religion and different philosophies around the world that people live by are there in the hopes of making people achieve the ultimate happiness. You must remember, this comes from within you, not from above you.

Through the years most of these important stories are lost in translation. We as a race, evolve, words change, meaning changes, but the intention stays the same. Books of myth, legend, religion, folklore and philosophy. Are they all different or are they kind of the same, just from a different time and space. If they are that different, what made one different from the other to you, and from the person writing it. Why does this part of the world have this view? Is it worth being right or wrong over?

When you see someone with a different belief than you, ask them about it, chances are they know more about it than you. If you are too afraid to ask, read and then read some more. Understand that part of the world, find out what other literature comes from that area, what films come from that area, what is the art in that area that is respected and appreciated by that group. What is important to that group of people today, that is different from your group of people and why. When you have a better understanding, you lose the idea of fear or anxiety from exhausting your energy on what you do not know, then you can have the courage to ask them face to face. To have a conversation. Maybe then you will see a similarity in beliefs and realize you are not that different in the spiritual sense. We are all humanity.

The more you read these different books that course through time and space, some of them will call to you a little bit more than others and that's ok. That call, is your heart, or some may say some form of spirit or intuition calling to you. Something about that book or poem grabbed a part of your soul and you felt it just as you feel your favorite song. Let it call, keep reading, because it will lead to being more curious. You will wonder, why did this make me feel that way. Dissect that feeling, force yourself to understand why. Sometimes you may not realize it yet, but that moment, in what you read, may become a significant part of your life. Because it will lead you to another book that changed your life immediately after, or 10 years later. Something may happen in your life that you do not understand, but for some reason, you remember that moment in that book and it hits you, you feel back in that moment, and now you understand the current situation. You will continue to learn and expand your mind, understanding more of the world over. The more of the world you understand with an open and curious mind the more you will start seeing these coincidences happening in your day to day life.

So many chase the idea of some form of spirit or ultimate beings that are running their lives. If they do this through ultimate righteousness, that's great, they are living the lives that many of these books are written about. If they are not living truly righteous, they are not doing what the book intends. They are living in fear of the consequences.

If we are all the children, why would I want my kids to worship me? I want to worship my kids. In a balanced and healthy way so they understand how much I truly love them more than anything else and want nothing but the best for them. I want my children to understand I am always here for you when you need me. I will do my best to give you amazing memories of this life. I want you to believe in yourself more than any other thing in the entire universe. I will support you, I will keep you safe, I will always be here, but I want you to chase your heart and be happy in this world. Let me know how I can help, I may not always be able to, but I will try. Yes, I may be stern at times, but are you listening? Let me talk so I may help you. Let me listen so I may help you.

VIII

Understand education can also be and often is a job in its own. They say if you love your job, you never have to work a day in your life. This is very true, but to what extent will you go to make this happen? As I said prior, when you follow your heart, you follow success. When you enjoy something in your heart you simply enjoy everything about that subject. Learning that subject is easy because it is fun, and you are learning to be the version of you that your soul wants.

Some things we do for the end goal, but we must have balance in that goal. Do you dislike your job but it provides you the life you want and that is enough for you to be content. Do you love your job but it does not afford the lifestyle you think you need? Perhaps you need to reevaluate your priorities, are you being wasteful in your life, are you being lazy when it comes to work? Do you want a similar job that is better paying but you do not want to move to a different area? Where are the issues in your job at hand, what can be done to fix them? Sometimes a great career must come to an end to be happy.

I understand when life is hard and we do not like our job, we can feel very stuck in life. Feeling stuck in our job can also give us large amounts of anxiety. Again, revealing itself as depression, anger, sadness or many other forms. How do we make our change now. Can we attend school again, a trade school, or can we move up at work from here? We make excuses of why we cannot move forward, we simply stay put in a constant mindset of being lost. We must set goals, realistic goals, goals we can keep honestly with ourselves. That way piece by piece, bit by bit, we start getting our life back on track. Remember it may be hard now, but the moment it is over is when you realize you are just beginning and it was worth it all.

Those around you will understand your sacrifice of making a new life, they will appreciate you more for what you are doing. They will support you in a way that they know how. Some people can only offer moral support, but they are cheering you on. Do not expect help from others, those that love you will show themselves to you offering their help and not wanting anything in return. Those that do not offer you anything do not deserve your reward in the end.

It is hard to explain the feelings of losing people during this process. Is what you are working to obtain worth more to you than a friendship? Most likely not, but they are not understanding how important this is to you and that this comes first, play comes later. Unfortunately, people evolve at different rates. Do not be mad at them, speak to them with honesty. I must do this before I can do that.

The things you choose to do in life, you must do them with the mindset of a warrior. You of course do not need to be a warrior, but the mindset of one. What they do, they take pride in themselves and they do it for the love of others. It is the most extreme version of passion that shows their love for others. Give yourself this same view to the things you are drawn to love. Be tactful, graceful, precise, and more than anything else, be humble.

The moment you begin to chase material gain over your passion, you begin to lose yourself. Your career worsens. Your homelife worsens. Keep your balance. Let your success speak for itself, you owe it to no one but yourself. Your job now is to support those you care about to reach their success in the ways that you can.

IX

When is enough, enough. One of the hardest choices in life we make is the choice to keep or lose someone. Physically, mentally, emotionally, they are true tolls to our soul. Because of the investment I made, is much too important to lose and I deserve it, or you deserve it. Maybe we deserve it.

How do I know when I have tried everything that is possible and I know I cannot change this outcome? Sometimes we do not have that answer when the time comes. Sometimes the answer is right in front of us and we are too blind to notice. Do we have the any form of ability to change the outcome?

As you begin to realize your own struggles that you battle, the demons they speak of. You begin to realize the battles of others. We do not want to watch those we love hurt, so we jump to action as we as humans should simply do. What do you have in your tool box that can help that person. Is that person willing to accept your tool or are they too busy digging for their own tool telling you, I got it, I got it. At what point do you stop holding your hand out to them. When are they starting to weigh you down. When do you know that point in your life where you need to say good bye. I am still here, with the tool, but I can no longer hold it up for you waiting, there are things I must do as well. I mean no harm and I love you, more than I know how to explain.

But, maybe they just are not listening. Why are they not listening when you are offering the answer they need. Where are their priorities in the moment, why do they have that as the priority over what you offer them. Was it something you already failed to offer multiple times?

How many fits of anger can you present before it is too late? How many fits of anger can you deal with before it is too late? How many tears are enough. How much pain is too much pain. Perhaps the other person had the tool the whole time and never offered it when you needed it.

X

As you continue on your path. You will soon begin to notice the things in life you may call a coincidence. When you see these, examine them. Why is this a feeling you have. Do not chase this, but allow it to lead you in a positive light. Understand it and see where it leads. Although change can be very demanding it starts with the smallest things.

When you find your tribe, when you find your music, when you find your thing. These little things will continue to show in your world. The more they begin to happen, the more you begin to question if they are more than a coincidence.

Following these positive intentions that formed from feelings, many areas of our lives start to make sense. We look over our life again. We find the beauty in the pain of the past. We start to align symbols to this feeling, things we often see in life that draws us towards it. Why does it draw us towards it. When do we learn about it? Why do we learn about it? Do we ever find the real answer? Or do we just hope someone else is telling the truth?

As these events continue to unfold in your life, you will feel as if things are actually starting to spiral inward, in good ways. You will feel yourself in a mindset of gratitude while understanding the idea of living in the now, every day as you chase the happiness we are required to find. You are thinking about your future from the perspective of your past. You are finally seeing why it all makes sense and as soon as it all lines up. You realize the feeling of being a waterfall made of electricity and imagination with no beginning or end. You have gone inside of your own self and found it.

You found the one thing in this world so many so blindly chase. You solved the ultimate equation. In doing so you realized what mattered and what did not matter, where your priorities now lay. You know how to say hello and goodbye. You help when you are needed, not demanded.

You have found your righteous path on this journey. You are living the way you should be living this life, without fear, without creating the idea of hell in this life. While you are doing this, you realize you are moving towards success. You are happy with what your job allows you to do in your life. Maybe you chase that one passion you became really good at and it has led to success. You will remember everyone that has a reason for being in your journey. You will want this for them. You will want to help them succeed in any way you can because you trust them and you love them. At this point you have seen where others have not been. You know what priorities you can put with certain people.

In this single flash of life, the spiral goes directly to your mind, showing you all the good you have done and will continue to do. In this moment, you found that feeling. The ultimate feeling of love.

In this moment we realize we have found the highest power most of the world praises. However, we simultaneously realize that power, was never explained the way the masses understand it. It was just something chased without understanding. A true feeling, lost to generations of corrupt power, lost souls, sheep or the blind. There was only myself. The intense work I put into myself to try to live what I consider to be a good life. I did it. I did it myself. I am now beaming with pride and asking to let me show you a way. You will now help yourself by helping others, succeeding every day and being grateful every day. Maybe it was the Earth, maybe it was the Universe, maybe it was the highest power. However, I know what I did by myself, prove me wrong.

We immediately realize everything we have been chasing in these feelings or symbols actually meant nothing to the daily life we live. But could we have done it without these symbols? Duality.

We realize that the symbols we were chasing were only that. Nothing more, nothing less. What did these symbols mean to the people that made them? Because I now realize they mean nothing to me, or so I thought, maybe they did since they were there along the way. What should my symbol be?

There is a way, it is a way I cannot explain. But I hope this helps you along your path.

The end of this journey, or the beginning?

Thank you for coming this far with me. Now do the things you are supposed to do. Eat your fruit, it gives you extra energy from the earth and sun. Eat your vegetables to keep your physical body in order. Eat some meat here in there, get the extra protein from the animal before you, thank them. Thank the ones who cooked for you. Eat in excess when you are celebrating, celebrate because you had a really good day. When you start having more really good days, stop giving yourself the food treat, change your pot of gold to something different as need be. Because life is about balance, if you are ruining your physical body now, you will be in the hospital longer in the end. Keep your food simple, keep it from Earth, it's better for the system that our body was made to be around. Read, do puzzles, challenge your brain. Your brain is a muscle, if you don't use it, you lose it. Do better to protect yourself from disorders like dementia, Parkinson's and Alzheimer's. Hug your friends and family. Smile at strangers. Be weird. Sing loud when others will not. Follow your heart and your heart will lead you to success.

As I asked you to read this with an open mind, I ask you to take the things from this book that made you think, and search out what about that made you think, learn about it. In life keep your mind open, let us understand each other.

I know here at the end it may not look like much, but this book took an intense amount of pain to gain the knowledge I have received to compress and translate the words on these pages. Pain of rage, pain of tears, pain of loss, pain of being wrong, pain of even finding out sometimes my heart was right. I hope you could feel the pain, the healing, the power, the intention behind the words. As you set this book down, I hope you hand it to someone else that you think needs to read it, or keep it for notes, highlights, something maybe to go back to. I hope you learn to laugh at the beauty of pain, because if you have not yet, it only gets better from here. I wish you all the happiness you can create. Now, watch what happens next.

About the Author

Sidney Rigden, raised in Racine, WI, is a transformative writer with a foundation in philosophy, psychology, and mental health. His journey has been shaped by a love for the stars, the warmth of bonfires, and the pursuit of life's deepest questions. As a devoted father, his children are his greatest inspiration and joy. Sidney's experiences as an Iraq veteran and a paramedic have profoundly influenced his perspective on life and humanity, instilling in him a deep understanding of pain, resilience, compassion, and the human spirit.

Driven by a passion for helping others discover their best selves, Sidney's writing weaves together insights from his diverse experiences and the wisdom of great thinkers. He encourages individuals to embrace the unknown, face their fears, and undertake powerful experiences that can lead to personal transformation and a sense of divinity. His mission is to change the world by fostering a deeper connection to our shared humanity and empowering others to realize the immense power within themselves.

Printed in the USA
CPSIA information can be obtained
at www.ICGtesting.com
CBHW022207271124
18026CB00041B/672